D0507817

Aberdeenshire

3247432

SPARKY'S STEM GUIDE TO...

TANKS

BY KIRSTY HOLMES

BookLife
PUBLISHING

©2019
BookLife Publishing Ltd.
King's Lynn
Norfolk PE30 4LS

All rights reserved.
Printed in Malaysia.

A catalogue record for this
book is available from the
British Library.

ISBN: 978-1-78637-717-3

Written by:
Kirsty Holmes

Edited by:
Emilie Dufresne

Designed by:
Danielle Rippengill

All facts, statistics, web addresses and URLs in this book were verified as valid and accurate at time of writing.
No responsibility for any changes to external websites or references can be accepted by either the author or publisher.

Original idea by Harrison Holmes.

IMAGE CREDITS

All images are courtesy of Shutterstock.com, unless otherwise specified. With thanks to Getty Images, Thinkstock Photo and iStockphoto.
Cover – NotionPic, A–R–T, logika600, BiterBig, Sapann Design, Sira Anamwong, KostyaTimofeev. Sparky – NotionPic, Sapann Design, Sira Anamwong.
Peggy – NotionPic, Sira Anamwong. Grid – BiterBig. Driving School – Elegant Solution. 2 – KostyaTimofeev. 5 – Mascha Tace. 6 – Murad_Mammadov.
6 & 7 – KostyaTimofeev. 7 – Roman Panfilov, Borodatch. 8 & 9 – Murad_Mammadov, KostyaTimofeev. 10 – Icon Craft Studio, Mike McDonald, M-vector,
hvostik, OksanaOO, Elchin Jafarli. 11 – alekseiveprev, Murad_Mammadov. 12 & 13 – Milagli. 14 – KostyaTimofeev. 15 – Murad_Mammadov, Francois Poirier.
16 – Mascha Tace. 17 – Murad_Mammadov. 18 – BigAlBaloo. 19 – ONYXprj. 20 – Mascha Tace. 21 – ArtMalivanov, DRogatnev. 22 – Francois Poirier,
Icon Craft Studio. 23 – Murad_Mammadov, brown32.

CONTENTS

WORDS THAT LOOK LIKE this CAN BE FOUND IN THE GLOSSARY ON PAGE 24.

WELCOME TO DRIVING SCHOOL!

Atten-TION! I'm Jeremy Sparkplug, world-famous tank commander. You can call me Sparky. At ease, **recruits** – this is the Horses for Courses School of Motoring!

Today, you will be learning about some mean, green driving machines – tanks! So listen up, recruits. If you pass your tank test, you'll earn your Golden Horseshoe.

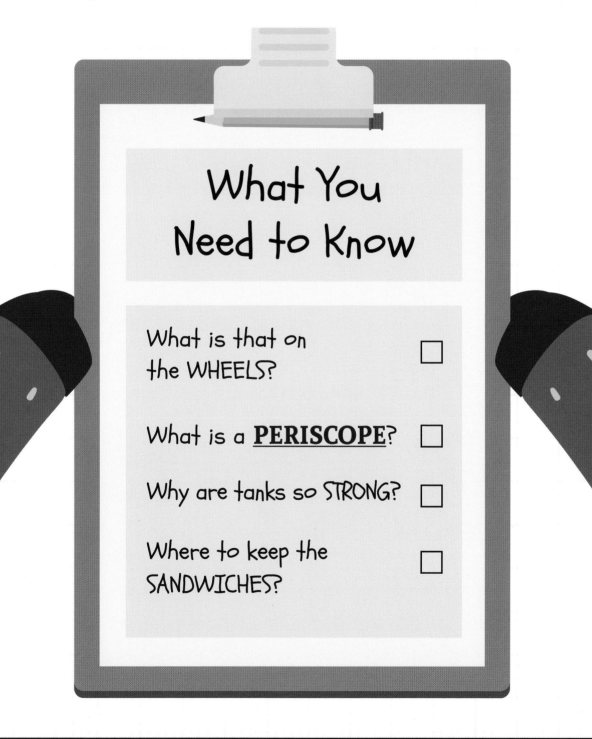

What You Need to Know

What is that on the WHEELS? ☐

What is a **PERISCOPE**? ☐

Why are tanks so STRONG? ☐

Where to keep the SANDWICHES? ☐

WHAT IS A TANK?

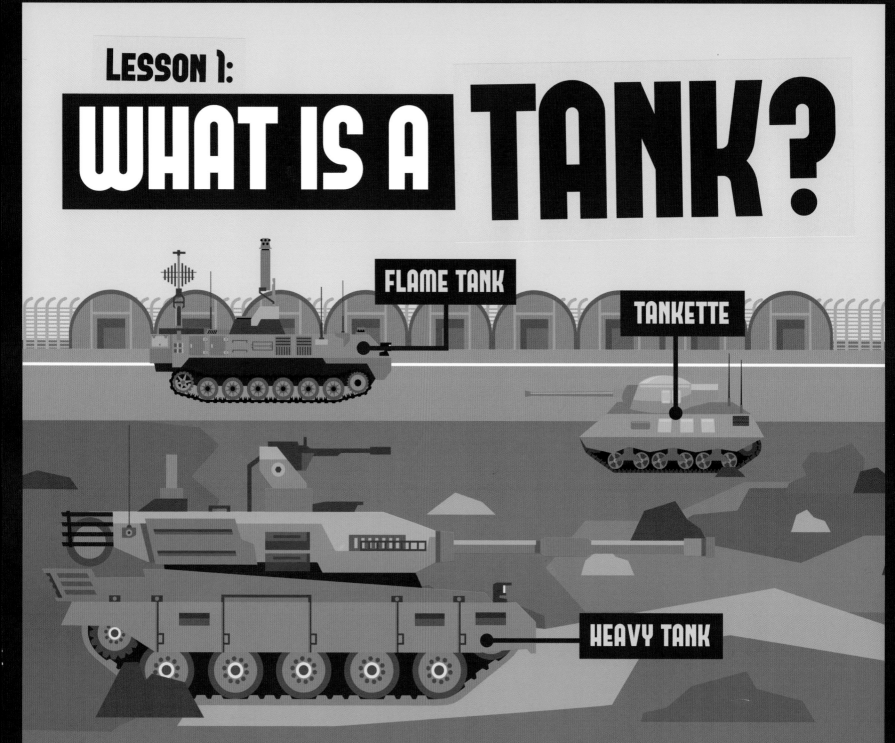

FLAME TANK

TANKETTE

HEAVY TANK

A tank is a <u>vehicle</u> used by the army. Tanks carry soldiers and weapons. They are used to protect soldiers and for attacking. They will usually have a heavy cannon and a few machine guns.

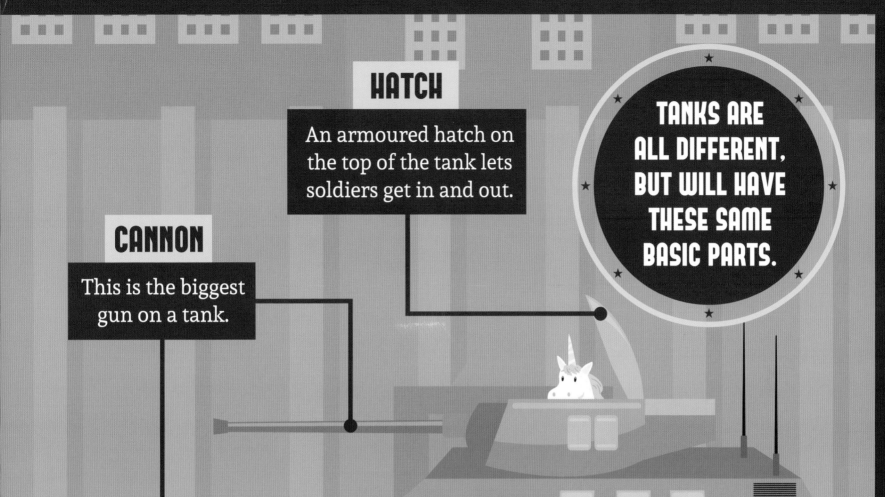

CANNON

This is the biggest gun on a tank.

HATCH

An armoured hatch on the top of the tank lets soldiers get in and out.

TANKS ARE ALL DIFFERENT, BUT WILL HAVE THESE SAME BASIC PARTS.

CATERPILLAR TRACKS

The wheels are inside these metal tracks. This means the wheels have something stable to drive on and don't get stuck in the mud.

HULL

The outside of the tank has heavy armour to protect it.

INSIDE A TANK

It's too small inside a tank to show you around so Peggy has taken everything out and put it here so you can have a look.

SIGHTS

These are for aiming the guns.

STEERING CONTROLS

Tanks turn by speeding up or slowing down one side of the tank. This is controlled using sticks and pedals.

PERISCOPE

Periscopes help the crew look around outside.

RADIO

People outside the tank tell the driver where to go.

FAN

Keeps you cool!

AMMUNITION

The bullets and **shells** are all stored in the tank.

Don't worry! These tanks are not **on duty** at the moment. There's no ammunition inside them today.

I keep my sandwiches in here. Marshmallow and pickle, my favourite!

CATERPILLAR TRACKS!

Tanks have to cross all kinds of **terrain**, such as sandy deserts, thick mud or ice and snow. Normal wheels would get stuck, or wouldn't be able to grip. Tank wheels are wrapped in a strip of metal plates, like this:

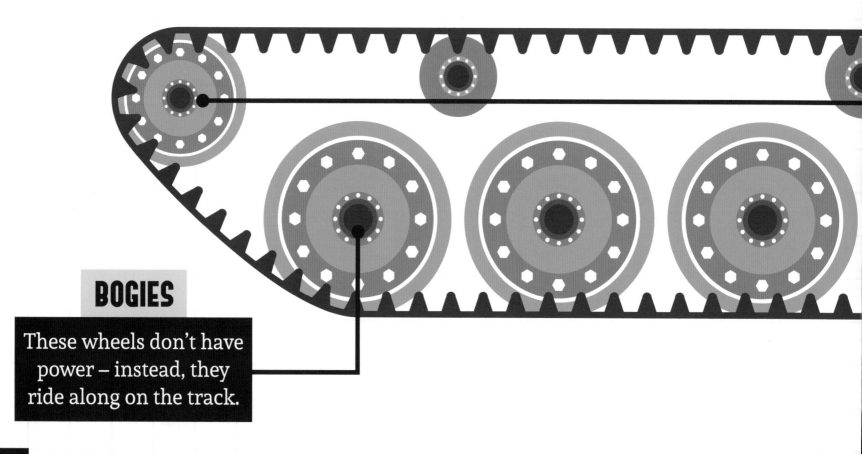

BOGIES

These wheels don't have power – instead, they ride along on the track.

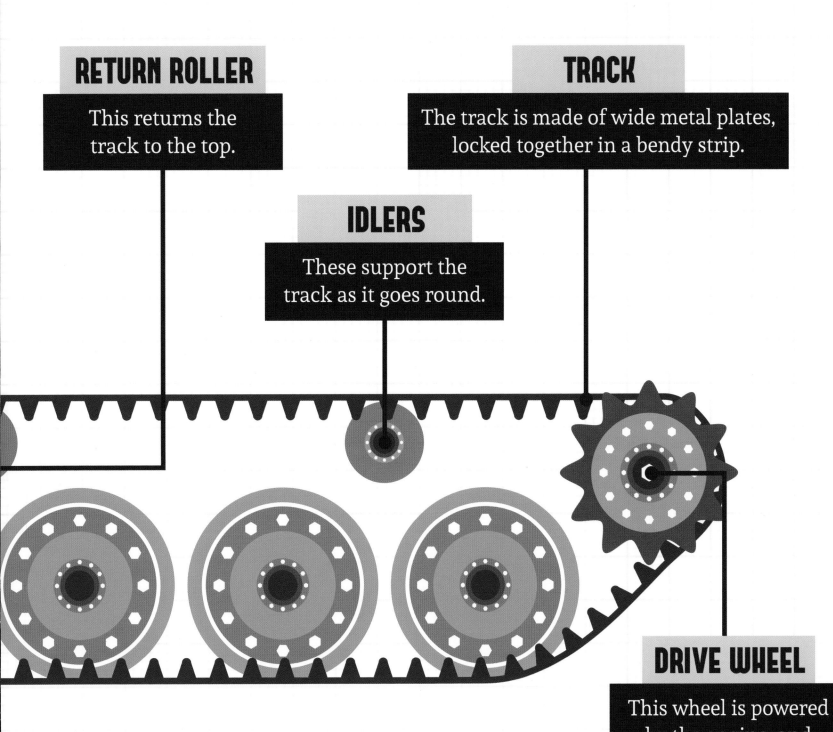

RETURN ROLLER

This returns the track to the top.

TRACK

The track is made of wide metal plates, locked together in a bendy strip.

IDLERS

These support the track as it goes round.

DRIVE WHEEL

This wheel is powered by the engine, and turns the track.

THE TURRET

The wheels and hull of a tank support the most important part – the turret. The tank's weapons are usually on the turret.

The turret can spin all the way around so that the gun can fire in all directions.

The tank commander sits inside the turret.
Sometimes the gunner will be in there too.
The commander's job is to tell the crew what
to do, where to go, and when the gunner should...

FIRE!!!

LESSON 6:
WHAT'S IN A NAME?

Why are tanks called, well, tanks? During World War I, the first tanks were built, and had to be kept secret. To do this, the British government pretended they were building **portable** water tanks. The name just stuck!

WATER TANK

Shhh!

Many types of tank have names. Tanks might be named after a famous person, such as the Churchill Mark VI which was named after the British Prime Minister during World War II, Winston Churchill.

THE HEAVIEST TANK EVER BUILT WAS CALLED THE MAUS WHICH IS GERMAN FOR MOUSE!

CHURCHILL MARK VI

TIP-TOP TANKS

MARK I FOSTER TANK

Made during World War I, this was one of the first ever tanks invented. Men used them to hide behind, and they were large enough to cross over deep trenches and squash enemy **barbed wire**.

PIGEONS

During the world wars, many tanks had holes in them for releasing pigeons! These trained pigeons could take messages back to the base asking for rescue.

A PIGEON CALLED WILLIAM OF ORANGE CARRIED A MESSAGE OVER 400 KILOMETRES AND SAVED 2,000 SOLDIERS!

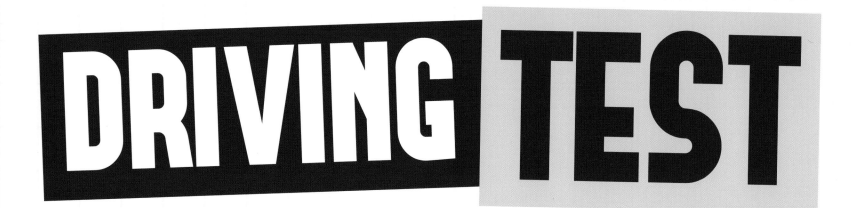

DRIVING TEST

Hoo-rah! Time for your tank test. Will you be able to hit all these questions on target?

Questions

1. What creatures are tank tracks named after?

2. What are sights for?

3. Where does the tank commander sit?

4. What did the British Government pretend they were building to keep the tanks secret?

5. How far did William of Orange fly with his distress message?

Did you get all the answers right?

Of course you did – here is your Golden Horseshoe.

You are now a Top Tank Commander, just like Peggy and me!

CANNONBALL!

Guns in position? Check.

Gunner ready – Peggy, that's you? Check! Cannon loaded? Check!

Time for... SPARKY CANNONBALL!

STEP ONE	STEP TWO	STEP THREE
Ready...	Take aim...	Fire!

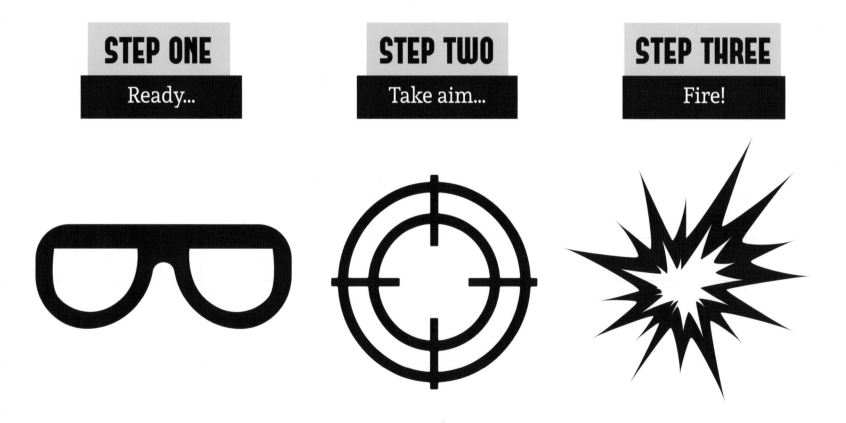

STEP FOUR

Look for a soft landing!

GLOSSARY

BARBED WIRE	a wire with barbs or spikes that is used to keep animals or people out of a certain place
ON DUTY	ready and available (military)
PERISCOPE	a tube that uses mirrors at each end to see things over an obstacle
PORTABLE	something that can be moved around easily
RECRUITS	new members of a group or organisation, such as the army, navy or air force
SHELLS	types of metal ammunition, which sometimes explode
TERRAIN	a type of land or ground
VEHICLE	a machine used for carrying or transporting things or people

INDEX